RHODE ISLAND

RHODE ISLAND

The Spirit of America

Text by Paula M. Bodah

Harry N. Abrams, Inc., Publishers

NEW YORK

This series was originated by Walking Stick Press, San Francisco
Series Designer: Linda Herman; Series Editor: Diana Landau

For Harry N. Abrams, Inc.:
 Editor: Nicole Columbus
 Designer: Ana Rogers

Photo research:
 Laurie Platt Winfrey, Leslie Van Lindt, Van Bucher
 Carousel Research, Inc.

Page 1: Sunset is a good time for crab hunting on a Portsmouth beach. *Photo Onne Van Der Wal/Stock Newport*
Page 2: *The Blue Porch* by Howard G. Cushing. 1909. *Newport Art Museum*

Library of Congress Cataloguing-in-Publication Data
Bodah, Paula M.
 Rhode Island : the spirit of America / text by Paula M. Bodah.
 p.   cm.
 ISBN 0–8109–5569–5
 1. Rhode Island—Civilization—Pictorial works.   2. Rhode Island—Miscellanea.
 I. Title. II. Series
F80.B63   2000
974.5'0022'2—dc21   00–029993

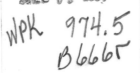

Harry N. Abrams, Inc.
100 Fifth Avenue
New York, N.Y. 10011
www.abramsbooks.com

A silk on silk needlework picture, possibly wrought by Louisa Gladding of Newport. *Christie's Images*

CONTENTS

Rhode Island wears its title as the smallest of the 50 states nobly. It has just 1,231 square miles to call its own, but so much about this tiny state is generous, from its great natural beauty to the vitality of its people to the ideals upon which it was founded.

It is also an enigmatic, quirky place. Those who live here feel an abiding love for and pride in their state, in spite of—or maybe because of —the fact that outsiders have often been blind to its special qualities. Cotton Mather in the 1600s called Rhode Island "the sewer of New England" because its settlers—a ragtag mix of eccentrics and rebels cast out of other colonies—welcomed people of diverse beliefs, including Quakers, Jews, and several offshoots of Puritanism. If religious tolerance was the colonists' most famous trait, it was also the manifestation of a deeper characteristic: their fervent individualism, which threads through more than three and half centuries of the state's history. Rhode Island's passion for self-rule made it the first of the 13 colonies to declare independence from Britain, the first to form a Continental navy, and the first to do battle with the British. That same independent streak led to the nickname "Rogue's Island," for its reluctance to join the new Union.

> "*The people of Rhode Island have it much in their hearts*
> to hold forth a lively experiment, that a flourishing and civil state
> may stand with a full liberty in religious commitments."
>
> *From the petition to King Charles II for a royal charter for the colony of Rhode Island*

As it became a geographically smaller part of an expanding nation, Rhode Island showed its spirit of self-determination by reinventing itself as an industrial powerhouse, launching the American Industrial Revolution on the banks of the Blackstone River near Providence. In the latter half of the 19th century, the state led the nation in manufacturing, producing more woolens and worsteds than any other state and ranking near the top in silver and costume jewelry manufacturing. Fruit of the Loom got its start here, as did Gorham Silver, the 19th century's largest producer of silverware.

Culturally, Rhode Island has always stood tall. In the 18th and 19th centuries, magnificent Colonial, Federal, and Victorian homes displayed fine furniture and silver crafted by local artisans. Narragansett Bay and its surrounding countryside inspired the best American painters, intellectuals, and writers of the day. John La Farge, John Frederick Kensett, and William Trost Richards depicted the landscape in many paintings; Edith Wharton and Henry James formed a lifelong friendship during summers on peaceful Aquidneck Island. Providence

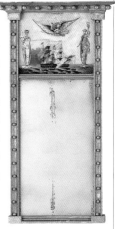

Federal giltwood and eglomise looking glass, labeled Peter Grinnell and Sons, Providence, 1809–c. 1812. *Christie's Images. Opposite: October Sundown, Newport, Rhode Island* by Childe Hassam, n.d. Hassam and other 19th-century painters found inspiration in Newport. *Art Resource, New York*

became a renowned center of higher learning with Brown University and the Rhode Island School of Design at its center. The list of contemporary artists, designers, writers, and musicians who have studied or taught at Brown or RISD includes fashion designer Nicole Miller, actor/songwriter Martin Mull, children's book author Chris Van Allsburg, and the rock group Talking Heads.

At the literal center of all that's important to Rhode Island is Narragansett Bay. It carves the state almost in half lengthwise, so that virtually every Rhode Islander lives on or near it. The bay is the state's spiritual lifeblood, the source of its greatest beauty. Away from the bay, too, the landscape is surprisingly unspoiled. Despite its small dimensions, the state has miles of rivers, farmland, hills, and forest for boating, bicycling, and hiking.

Socially, Rhode Island operates more like a city than a state. Nearly 70 percent of residents were born here, and family and friendship are paramount. Ethnic roots—whether Italian or African American, Irish or Asian, Portuguese or Latino—run deep for generations, bringing richness and vitality to the cultural terrain. The state's founder, Roger Williams, would be proud of his experiment in social diversity.

Rhode Island's chief gift may be its talent for survival. At every turn, whether threatened by war, economic decline, or natural disaster, its people have used their ingenuity and self-reliance to find new success. In the 20th century, the state found its way from manufacturing prominence to a new service-based economy, and today it's enjoying another renaissance. Magazines and newspapers praise it as a great place to vacation, to raise children, to get a fine meal; writers and filmmakers have discovered it makes a perfect setting. Celebrities have quietly bought vacation homes along its waterfront. The hit TV show *Providence* shows off the capital city's architecture, and recent

movies such as *There's Something About Mary* (from native sons Peter and Bobby Farrelly) and Steven Spielberg's *Amistad* have been filmed here.

Those who live here awelcome visitors, new families, and movie stars. They get a kick out of seeing Bristol homeowner Anthony Quinn at a Federal Hill market, or knowing they might run into frequent visitor Billy Joel dining at Providence's star restaurant Al Forno. But they don't need outsiders to prove their state's worth. They know that Rhode Island is the nation's biggest (in this way, at least) and best-kept secret. ◉

American Eagle sails through Newport's inner harbor, with the city as a backdrop.
Photo Onne Van Der Wal/Stock Newport

RHODE ISLAND

"The Ocean State"

13th State

Date of Statehood
MAY 4, 1790

Capital
PROVIDENCE

Bird
RHODE ISLAND RED HEN

Flower
VIOLET

Tree
RED MAPLE

Shellfish
QUAHOG

Fruit
RHODE ISLAND
GREENING APPLE

Rock
CUMBERLANDITE

Standing atop the State House, the Independent Man unofficially symbolizes the proud spirit of a place unique for much more than its tiny dimensions.

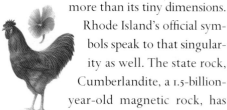

Violet and Rhode Island Red hen

Rhode Island's official symbols speak to that singularity as well. The state rock, Cumberlandite, a 1.5-billion-year-old magnetic rock, has been found nowhere outside the state's borders. Nearly as hard to find elsewhere is the state beverage—coffee milk—a concoction Rhode Island children are weaned on. The state shellfish, called *Mercenaria* from the Latin for money because Native Americans cut and polished its shell into wampum, is better known as the quahog (pronounced *KO-hog*). The Rhode Island Red hen, famed for its brown eggs, ruled the roost in the poultry industry at one time. And the capital city of Providence has been dressed up with a new downtown—a shining symbol of Rhode Island's reclaimed reputation as New England's oceanside gem. ◉

"Hope"

*State motto; derived from Roger Williams's
"hope in the divine" to see him through the
first harsh winter in Rhode Island*

State Capitol, Providence, R. I.

Fowl Play

No soaring eagle, no
sweet-throated mead-
owlark can match the
Rhode Island Red hen for
sheer utility. The state
bird was developed in 1854
by a Little Compton
farmer, who let an Asian
red cock run with his

The state capitol in
Providence, designed by
the well-known archi-
tectural firm of McKim,
Mead and White and
built in 1898, boasts the
fourth-largest unsup-
ported marble dome in
the world. *Culver Pictures
Left:* Rhode Island Red
rooster. *Photo Rod
Planck/Photo Researchers,
Inc.*

scrub hens and noticed that their offspring were more robust
and laid more and bigger eggs. By the early 20th century, the
Red, with its distinctive brown eggs, was a mainstay of the
commercial poultry industry. In 1925, a monument honoring
the hardy breed—supposedly the world's only monument to
a chicken—was erected in Little Compton.

A Tale of Two Jonnycakes

Narragansett Bay cleaves Rhode Island almost in half, south to north, and those who live on either side of the bay harbor an abiding belief in their side's superiority. The question of how to cook a perfect jonnycake is a case in point. All agree it must be made from Rhode Island flintcap corn meal, but West Bay natives prefer a plump cake made by pouring just enough scalding water on the cornmeal to make a thick, doughy mixture. East-siders use cold milk for a runny batter, producing wafer-thin pancakes with lacy brown edges. Here is an East Bay recipe. You may smother yours in syrup; Rhode Islanders prefer a pat of butter or a dollop of jam.

1/2 tsp. salt
1 tsp. sugar
1 cup Rhode Island (or white) cornmeal
1¾ cups milk
Butter for frying

Combine sugar, salt, and cornmeal. Add milk and mix thoroughly. Melt some butter in a skillet and pour batter in, letting it spread to make a cake about 3 in. diameter. Cook until top is set, then flip and cook for another minute or so. Add more milk as needed to keep batter at the proper thin consistency. Makes a dozen jonnycakes.

Although Rhode Island's official state song is **"Rhode Island's It for Me"** (words by Charlie Hall, music by Maria Day), the 1948 song **"Rhode Island Is Famous for You"** by Howard Dietz and Arthur Schwartz boasts a catchier tune and lyrics. Here's a sampling:

Every state has something its Rotary Club
    can boast of,
Some product that the state produces the
    most of.
Rhode Island is little, but oh, my
It has a product anyone would buy:

Copper comes from Arizona
Peaches come from Georgia
And lobsters come from Maine.
The wheat fields are the sweet fields of
    Nebraska
And Kansas gets bonanzas from the grain.
Old whisky comes from old Kentucky.
Ain't the country lucky New Jersey gave
    us blue?
And you, you come from Rhode Island
And little old Rhode Island is famous for you.

"What Cheer, Netop."

The greeting with which the Narragansett Indians are said to have welcomed Roger Williams when he arrived in the place he called Providence, in 1636

Horses of Another Color

There are older carousels in America but
none so stunning as the Crescent Park
Carousel, in East Providence. Charles I.
D. Looff, the famed Danish carousel
builder, set up shop here and in 1895 built
a carousel that doubled as his showroom:
66 of the finest horses he ever carved,
along with a couple of dragon-pulled
chariots and a single camel (so the ticket-
taker knew where to start and end).
Today the refurbished carousel is Rhode
Island's official folk art symbol. It spins
around its original calliope at a speedy 14
mph, daring riders to risk a one-handed
grab for the gold ring and a free ride.

Pick on Someone Your Own Size

The smallest state is a convenient yardstick.
Witness these reference to things the size of
Rhode Island.

"[The dinosaurs] kind of got in the way of a
whopping great meteorite half the size of
Rhode Island . . . ."

The Providence Journal

". . . a glass or two of champagne . . . and a
really big cigar, about the size of Rhode Island.
Now there's a truly delightful and delicious
experience."

The Seattle Times

"This satellite picture shows an iceberg the
size of Rhode Island cracking away from
Antarctica."

Dateline NBC

"It's time to drink beer from vats the size of
Rhode Island."

Miller Beer TV ad

"The fouled water flow has spawned an algae
bloom the size of Rhode Island . . . killing
North America's only coral reefs."

From an article in *The Nation*

RHODE ISLAND MILESTONES

c. 1200 A.D. Asiatic peoples, ancestors of the Wampanoag and Narragansett tribes, settle in area.

1524 Giovanni da Verrazano makes first verifiable visit by a European to Rhode Island.

1614 Dutch explorer Adriaen Block visits; names Block Island for himself.

1635 First permanent white settler, William Blackstone, moves to what is now the Blackstone River, in Pawtucket.

1636 Roger Williams leaves Massachusetts Bay colony seeking religious freedom; founds Providence.

1638 Anne Hutchinson, only woman to found a colonial town, establishes Portsmouth on Aquidneck Island.

1639 America's First Baptist Church formed, in Providence.

1657 Quakers establish first Meeting House, in Newport.

1675 Some 700 Narragansett Indians killed by colonists in the Great Swamp Fight during King Philip's War.

1726 James Franklin (Ben's brother), moves to Newport and begins publishing colony's first newspaper, the *Rhode Island Gazette.*

1736 Touro Synagogue, oldest synagogue in North America, built in Newport.

1764 Rhode Island College, later renamed Brown University, founded.

1769 Colonists burn the British revenue schooner *Gaspee* in the waters off Warwick.

1776 Rhode Island is first colony to declare independence from Britain.

1786 Bristol holds first Fourth of July Parade, now the nation's oldest.

1789 Capt. Robert Gray of Tiverton completes first circumnavigation of the globe by an American.

1790 Rhode Island is last of the 13 colonies to ratify U.S. Constitution.

1790 Samuel Slater, the "Father of American Manufacturing," builds first water-powered cotton-spinning mill in U.S., in Pawtucket.

1815 The Great Gale, a violent hurricane, hits Rhode Island, flattening hundreds of homes and destroying scores of ships, but, miraculously, killing only seven people.

1835 State's first railroad, the Boston and Providence, begins operation.

1843 State constitution formally abolishes slavery.

1854 William Tripp breeds first Rhode Island Red chicken.

1854 Providence and Newport named Rhode Island's co-capitals.

1866 General Assembly outlaws racial segregation in the public schools.

1876 Providence inventor George Corliss's giant steam engine powers all the machinery at the Philadelphia Centennial Exposition.

1877 Rhode Island School of Design founded.

1884 Naval War College at Newport opens.

1892 William K. Vanderbilt builds Marble House, one of the first of Newport's famous "summer cottages."

1893 Racing yacht *Vigilant*, built by Herreshoff Manufacturing Co., becomes the first of five Herreshoff yachts to win America's Cup.

1894 Knight brothers form Fruit of the Loom textile mill.

1900 Providence becomes the sole capital and leads U.S. in production of woolen and worsted goods.

1905 Census reveals the state is more than 50 percent Roman Catholic; first Catholic governor, James H. Higgins, elected the next year.

1914 Johnson and Wales, today the world's largest culinary school, founded.

1918 George M. Cohan of Providence writes "Over There," the unofficial WWI anthem.

1922 Rhode Island's first female state legislator elected.

1929 Mount Hope Bridge built, linking Aquidneck Island to mainland.

1930 Newport becomes the site of the America's Cup races.

1938 A hurricane, the state's worst natural disaster, kills 311.

1943 First Quonset hut built at North Kingstown's Quonset Point Naval Air Station.

1969 Former governor John H. Chafee named secretary of the navy. Newport Bridge links southern end of Aquidneck with Jamestown, ending the oldest continuous ferry service in the nation.

1980 Congresswoman Claudine Schneider becomes first Rhode Island woman elected to national office.

1981 Pawtucket Red Sox, Boston Red Sox farm team, hosts (and wins) longest professional baseball game: 30 innings.

1986 The state and the city of Providence celebrate 350th anniversary.

1987 Providence hosts the first X Games, televised on ESPN.

1998 The Farrelly brothers, of Cumberland, shoot the hit movie *There's Something About Mary* in Rhode Island.

Block Island's Great Salt Pond and the Champlin Farm sweep toward Block Island Sound. Ten miles in the distance is the Rhode Island mainland. *Photo Malcolm Greenaway*

Rhode Island earns its nickname, the Ocean State, from the 384 miles of shoreline that lace the state's southern border and outline Narragansett Bay as it slices into the land northward from the coast. Along the southern shore, beginning at the Connecticut border, mile follows mile of unspoiled beach and wide ocean vistas. At Newport, the Atlantic Ocean churns against a craggy shoreline built of massive, half-billion-year-old rocks deposited

15 millennia ago by an Ice Age glacier. Islands large and small dot the bay as it makes its way inland. To the north and west of Providence, vestiges of the state's days as an industrial powerhouse still show in the mill villages along the banks of the rivers and ponds that take up 168 square miles of the state's meager 1,231. Although this is one of the country's most densely populated states, a ten-minute drive

from Providence leads to a surprising wealth of woods-studded rolling hills and farmland, and Rhode Island's highest point—Jerimoth Hill—all of 812 feet. ◉

North Light, a functioning lighthouse that houses a small museum, sits on Block Island's northern tip. *Photo Malcolm Greenaway. Left:* Newport's Cliff Walk winds along for a mile and a half, with views of First Beach, seen here, and the Atlantic Ocean on one side, and the backyards of the opulent mansions on the other. *Photo Allison Langley/Stock Newport*

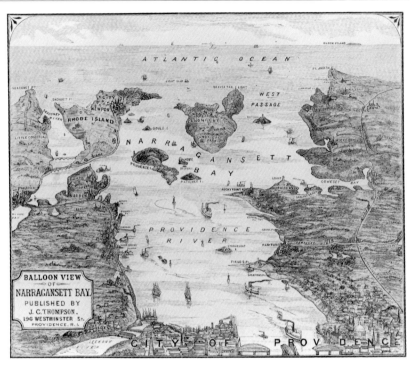

A panoramic view of
Narragansett Bay in
1882 illustrates the
importance of the bay
for both commerce and
recreation. More than
30 islands, large and
small, are scattered
throughout the bay.
*Rhode Island Historical
Society*

Waters of Life

Narragansett Bay is not only Rhode Island's jewel but its heart
and soul. Some 15,000 years ago, a glacier gashed the land, leav-
ing the bay as its legacy. By 6500 B.C., when the first people
arrived, the waters teemed with life—including oysters the
size of dinner plates—making it a choice spot to settle. The
bay has been the lifeblood of those who live here ever since.

For the colonists, it was a trade route to commercial prosperity. Today the bay remains vital to the state's economy, bringing in $750 million a year from fishing and generating much of the $2.5 billion in annual tourism revenues.

But the bay's spiritual contribution might be more important. No Rhode Islander lives more than a half hour's drive from its shore, and many crisscross it daily on a network of bridges. All that water made travel a challenge in earlier times, encouraging a regionalism that still yields variety and richness. Where you're from—upstate or downstate, island or mainland, East Bay or West Bay—can determine matters from your accent to how you like your chowder. Still, even as it separates them physically, Narragansett Bay unites Rhode Islanders in their awe of its beauty and preciousness.

Commercial fishermen hoist the catch of the day, in the waters off of Newport. *Photo Onne van der Wal/Stock Newport*

Miles of Isles

Newport in its early days was as much a farming town as a merchant port, as seen in *Old Homestead by the Sea* by Worthington Whittredge, c. 1872. *Courtesy Adelson Galleries, Inc.*

The littlest state has the biggest official name: Rhode Island and Providence Plantations. The island now called Aquidneck —with three towns and 64,594 people on its 43.9 square miles— is the "Rhode Island" part of that name. Narragansett Bay is studded with 38 islands big and small, from well-populated ones like Aquidneck, best known for Newport at its southern end, to tiny islets that are little more than slabs of rock sticking up out of the bay; from the lyrically named Patience, Rose, and Hope to the colorfully named Fox, Hog, and Goat. Block Island, a favorite getaway for political and Hollywood celebrities, lies ten miles off the mainland's south shore. Some 5,000 people live on Conanicut Island, better known as the town of Jamestown, whereas Prudence is a year-round home to only the hardiest. Dutch Island, named for his country by the 17th-century explorer Adriaen Block (who immodestly named Block Island, too), is the site of an abandoned World War II fortification. Besides making a picturesque landscape, the islands are home to abundant wildlife, including at least 40 species of birds that use them as migration points.

"[THE RHODE ISLAND] CLIMATE IS LIKE THAT OF ITALY, AND NOT AT ALL colder in the winter than I have known it everywhere north of Rome. The spring is late, but to make amends they assure me the autumns are the finest and longest in the world, and the summers are much pleasanter than those of Italy by all accounts, for as much as the grass continues green . . . ."

Bishop Berkeley, in a 1729 letter

Map of Rhode Island, 17th century. *Rhode Island Historical Society. Below:* William Trost Richards painted many landscapes of Newport and its surroundings, including this painting, *The Old Fort, Conanicut Island,* an 1877 view of a Revolutionary War fortification. Conanicut Island, also known as Jamestown, sits in Narragansett Bay just west of Newport. *Wadsworth Athenaeum, Hartford*

Rivers Run Through It

In the early 1800s mill towns sprang up along northern Rhode Island's Blackstone River, which became one of the most heavily industrialized waterways in the nation. This 1830s print of an engraving by J. S. Lincoln shows mill villages in North Providence and Pawtucket. *Rhode Island Historical Society*

The bay gets most of the attention in Rhode Island, but a good handful of rivers thread through woods, farmland, even cities. The Blackstone River, which flows down from Massachusetts, is queen of the state's rivers. Once among the nation's most polluted waterways—thanks to Rhode Island's industriousness—the now pure Blackstone welcomes kayaks and tour boats filled with weekend adventurers. The Moshassuck and Woonasquatucket, paved over by urban planners of previous generations, have been uncovered and redirected to flow through Providence's newly refurbished downtown. In the southern part of the state, the Narrow, Wood, and Pawcatuck

Rivers wind past 18th-century farmhouses and mill villages, honoring a time long gone.

That Rhode Island has so much rural acreage is a surprise; it is, after all, the second most densely populated state. Several hundred dairy farms, potato farms, apple orchards, and nurseries still thrive, as well as a handful of centuries-old working farms that use colonial-era farming methods. In the past decades, the state has purchased some 3,000 acres of land for open space preservation, so Rhode Islanders can count on seeing green for generations to come.

A speedboat races down the Pawcatuck River.
Photo Alison Langley/ Stock Newport

Roger Williams opposing the Pequot emissaries. *Culver Pictures Right:* **Giovanni da Verrazano sailed into Narragansett Bay in 1524, earning credit as the first European explorer to chart the bay.** *American Heritage/Pierpont Morgan Library, New York*

Natives and Newcomers

Newport calls itself "America's First Resort"—and it just might be true, judging from archaeological evidence. Prehistoric Asiatic people apparently summered along Rhode Island's southern coast as much as 8,000 years ago, retreating to the thick inland forests for winter protection. By the 1520s, when Giovanni da Verrazano made the first verifiable visit to Rhode Island by a European, a number of Algonquian tribes were firmly ensconced in the area. One of the largest of these were the Narragansett, who were friendly to the explorers, guiding Verrazano's ship into harbor and playing host to him while he charted the bay waters. Historians estimate that 7,000 Narragansett lived in Rhode Island at this time. Before the end of the 17th century, nearly every Narragansett was dead, killed by European diseases and bitter fighting with the new settlers. Today, descendants of those Native Americans hold about 2,500 acres of ancestral land in the southern part of the state—but their ancestors' legacy reaches far beyond that meager allotment, enriching Rhode Island culture in innumerable ways.

By the end of the 17th century, the Narragansett Indians had been largely wiped out by disease and war with the European settlers. Ninigret II, shown in this portrait, assumed leadership of the small group of Narragansett who survived. *Artist and date unknown. Photo courtesy Rhode Island School of Design Museum of Art*

I've known them to leave their house and mat
to lodge a friend or stranger.
When Jews and Christians oft have sent
Christ Jesus to the Manger.

Roger Williams, writing about Massasoit and the Wampanoag Indians

NEWPORT, R.I. IN 1730.

SHIPPING HORSES wanted.

NICHOLAS BROWN,
and COMPANY,
Want to buy immedi-
ately, a few likely SURINAM HORSES.

Colonial Prosperity

Life was good in colonial Rhode Island. Shortly after Roger Williams founded Providence in 1636, disputes among his followers led in quick succession to the founding of Portsmouth and Newport on Aquidneck Island, and Warwick on the west side of the bay. By the end of the 1600s, Newport was a prosperous port—due in no small part to its participation in the Triangle Trade, through which Rhode Island achieved the dubious distinction of having more slaves per capita than any other New England colony. By the mid-1700s, the city was also known for the talents of its fine furniture makers. Meanwhile, Williams was buying up property from the Indians until Providence comprised 380 square miles, extending north and east to Massachusetts and west to the Connecticut border. The southwestern half of the colony, with its abundant farmland

and ample black and Indian slave labor, became a leading exporter of lumber and livestock—notably the now-extinct Narragansett Pacer, a carriage horse breed prized by Caribbean plantation owners.

Gilbert Stuart, an important portraitist of the 18th century (his portrait of George Washington adorns the $1 bill), painted this portrait of a Newport woman, Mrs. Bannister, and her son, in 1774. *Redwood Library and Athenaeum, Newport*

America's First Feminist

Like Roger Williams, Anne Hutchinson was kicked out of the Massachusetts Bay Colony for her heretical beliefs, as she held that salvation came from faith rather than obedience to church or civil law. In 1638, she founded the town of Portsmouth—the only Colonial town founded by a woman—on the north end of Aquidneck Island, giving the island a reputation as a haven for religious dissenters. Always restless, Hutchinson didn't stay long. In 1642, after her husband's death, she moved to New York. One year later, she and five of her 14 children were killed in an Indian massacre.

Landung einer Französischen Hülfs Armee in America, zu Rhode Island am 11ten Julius 1780.

Independent First and Last

Rhode Island threw itself into the American Revolution. In June 1772, a year and a half before Bostonians conducted their famous Tea Party, Providence citizens attacked and burned the British sloop *Gaspee* off Warwick, in one of the first overt acts of rebellion against the Crown. On May 4, 1776, Rhode Island became the first colony to declare independence. Rhode Island created the first Colonial navy, and in 1775 the *Katy,* built by prominent Providence businessman John Brown and later renamed *Providence,* won the first official battle of the war. Later that year, Esek Hopkins, also of Providence, was appointed the first commander in chief of the U.S.

General Jean Baptiste Rochambeau and the French army arrived in Rhode Island on July 11, 1780, to help the Colonies fight the British. Engraving by D. Berger, 1784. *Library of Congress. Right*: Oliver Hazard Perry, naval hero and commander of the American forces that defeated the British at the Battle of Lake Erie during the War of 1812, and Hannibal Collins (center rear) at the Battle of Lake Erie. *Newport Historical Society*

Navy. Rhode Island's truest hero of the revolution, though, was Warwick's Nathanael Greene, a quartermaster general under George Washington whose brilliant military tactics set up Cornwallis for his fall at Yorktown. Yet for all its revolutionary zeal, Rhode Island refused to approve the Constitution. Quakers opposed its implicit approval of slavery, farmers rejected it fearing big land taxes, and Rhode Islanders in general distrusted big government. Finally, in May 1790, by a two-vote margin, Rhode Island became the last of the 13 colonies to join the Union.

In June 1772, Rhode Islanders committed the first overt act of aggression against the British by burning the British sloop *Gaspee* in Narragansett Bay. *Burning of the Gaspee* by D. W. Brownell, 1892. *Rhode Island Historical Society*

EL RHODE ISLAND ENTRANDO EL CORTE DE CULEBRA, CANAL DE PANAMA.

228B. U.S.S. RHODE ISLAND PASSING CULEBRA CUT, PANAMA CANAL.

The U.S.S. Rhode Island is shown in the Panama Canal on this postcard. *Corbis. Right:* The first torpedo built by the Naval Torpedo Station in Newport, in 1871, had 100 pounds of dynamite and could travel 200 yards at a speed of six to eight knots. *Naval War College Museum*

State of the Navy

Rhode Island's association with the U.S. Navy is a long and proud one. At the start of the Revolutionary War, Providence's Esek Hopkins was named the first commander in chief of the continental navy. Oliver Hazard Perry of South Kingstown commanded the fleet that won the Battle of Lake Erie during the War of 1812, and his son Matthew C. Perry led the historic 1853 expedition that opened Japan to trade with the West. From 1869 through the 1940s, Newport was home to the nation's largest producer of torpedoes. At Quonset Point Naval Air Station, on the west side of Narragansett Bay, the first of the famous Quonset huts was built in 1941; here, too, the navy's first jet fighter squadron was

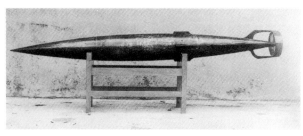

> ## "We have met the enemy and they are ours."
>
> *Oliver Hazard Perry, Rhode Island sailor and commander of the fleet that won the Battle of Lake Erie in the War of 1812, in a note to General William Henry Harrison*

Recruits at the Newport Naval Training Station in 1917 used mattresses as life preservers. *Corbis*

formed and trained. The glory years ended abruptly in 1974, when President Richard Nixon pulled much of the fleet out of Newport. Sixteen thousand civilians lost their jobs, and the Aquidneck Island town of Middletown lost 41 percent of its population. Today, despite a vastly reduced fleet presence, Newport is still the center of naval education, thanks largely to the renowned Naval War College, which opened in 1884.

Folding the Run by Penelope Manzella, 1989, depicts the Griswold Textile Factory in Westerly. *Courtesy of the Artist. Below:* Benjamin and Robert Knight's textile manufacturing company, which included Fruit of the Loom, was among the largest textile businesses in the world as the 20th century began. *Rhode Island Historical Society*

In colonial times, Rhode Island's wealth came from both ocean and land. The Triangle Trade turned sugar and slaves into big business. Although other colonies got richer on fishing and whaling, Rhode Island cornered the market on a byproduct from whaling. Using spermaceti—which sailors believed was whale sperm but was actually a substance from the whale's head—workers made a high-quality candle that was much in demand, and Rhode Island became the colonies' leading manufacturer of candles. The forests, farms, and plantations in South County turned lumber, sheep, dairy products, apples, onions, and flax into wealth, building a busy trade with England, Africa, South America, and the West Indies.

As the nation grew, Rhode Island couldn't compete as a farming state for long. But its entrepreneurial spirit lived on into statehood and—aided by an intricate system of rivers north and west of Providence—led to its next big success, in the textiles industry. In 1790 Samuel Slater built a water-powered cotton-spinning mill in Pawtucket, sparking America's Industrial Revolution. For the next century, the state played a dominant role in the textile industry; in 1900 Providence produced more woolens and worsted than any other city in the nation. ◉

Workers at Hasbro, the world's second-largest toy company, crank out some of the most popular toys ever, including G.I. Joe and Mr. Potato Head. *Corbis.*

The Cost of Progress

The first American workers' strike occurred in Rhode Island in 1800, when weavers at Samuel Slater's cotton mill walked off their jobs. Used to doing piecework at home, they resented working under supervision for upward of 60 hours a week. But the weavers couldn't stop technology, and factory work became the livelihood of most Rhode Islanders.

From Farm to Factory

Factories need machines and tools, which triggered a boom in the metals industry. Metals production, in turn, spurred a whole new industry in jewelry and silverware. By 1860, with only 10 percent of its people still working in agriculture, Rhode Island had become the most industrialized state in the country. Metals manufacturing, especially in the costume jewelry industry, still figures largely in the local economy. Some 25 percent of the nation's costume jewelry workers live and work here, making everything from earring backs to Miss America's tiara.

Doing Business

Big names in Rhode Island business span many eras and industries. **A.T. Cross** was founded in 1846 as America's first maker of fine pens and other writing instruments. George Corliss of Providence patented a revolutionary steam engine design; his **Corliss Steam Engine Company** (est. 1848) was the nation's largest steam engine factory, and its engine powered all the machinery at the 1876 Philadelphia Centennial Exposition. The **Fruit of the Loom** underwear firm, opened in 1895 by the Knight brothers, at its peak employed 7,000 people. The mill went bankrupt in 1924, but the name was bought by the out-of-state Union Underwear Company in 1938 and lives on. **GTECH,** the world's biggest online lottery company with annual revenues of almost $1 billion, started in 1981 and now installs and services 80 lottery systems in 34 countries. **Gorham Silver,** founded in 1813, was the country's largest manufacturer of silverware through the 19th century. Gorham cast the Independent Man, which stands on the State House dome. Pawtucket-based **Hasbro** is the world's second-largest toy company; its famous toys include Mr. Potato Head and G.I. Joe. It also holds the exclusive license for Star Wars toys. And the worldwide conglomerate **Textron,** based in Providence, ranks 149th on the Fortune 500. Among its holdings are Bell Helicopter and the Cessna Aircraft Company.

Among the 60 patents held by inventor George Corliss was one for his 1848 invention of this steam engine with an automatic cutoff valve. *Smithsonian Institution, Washington, D.C. Below:* A 1927 silver "Cubic" coffee service, designed by Erik Magnussen, from the Gorham Silver Company. Founded in 1813, Gorham was the country's largest producer of silverware in the 19th century. The company also cast the Independent Man statue that stands atop the Statehouse. *Museum of Art, Rhode Island School of Design*

Fish Stories

Fishing trawlers alongside the docks at Galilee, one of Rhode Island's busiest commercial fishing ports. *Photo Allison Langley/Stock Newport*

Legend says that the Indians welcomed Roger Williams by inviting him to share a meal of fish and succotash. Rhode Islanders have been thriving on local seafood ever since. Throughout the 18th and 19th centuries, fishing—especially shellfishing—was a big business in the state. Whole villages, like Scalloptown on the west side of Narragansett Bay, sprang up around the shellfish industry. At the start of the 20th century, a thousand harvesters pulled 15 million pounds of oysters from the bay each year. The shellfish population isn't nearly so bountiful as it once was, but Narragansett Bay oysters, scallops, and clam are still prized for their delicate flavor, and hundreds

still make a living from bay shellfishing. Fin fishermen ply the off-shore waters, catching bluefish, cod, and mackerel for export, as well as giant bluefin tuna, swordfish, white marlin, and striped bass. Today, fishing in Rhode Island is a $750 million business annually. Most of the catch—about 85 percent—is exported to other states and overseas.

Squid Pro Quo

Rhode Island probably consumes more squid, or *calamari,* than any other state. It's used in many forms, from infusing its ink into fresh pasta to frying it with hot-pepper relish—a local favorite. To make fried *calamari,* buy cleaned squid bodies from your fish market. Slice into rings about ¼-in. thick (cut any clumps of tentacles into halves or quarters). Dredge the rings and tentacles in beaten egg, then in flour; fry in about ½ in. of oil for just a minute or two (too long makes squid tough). Drain on paper towels and serve immediately with hot-pepper relish.

Bass fisherman at Bateman's Hotel. *Newport Historical Society.* **Above: Gathering quahogs is still done the old-fashioned way, by bullrake, along the Rhode Island coast.** *Photo Stock Boston*

The 84-inch-long, poly-chromed wood stern-board of the *Eunice H. Adams*. The boat was built in Bristol in the mid-1800s and used in the whaling trade out of New Bedford, Massachusetts. *Old Dartmouth Historical Society, New Bedford Whaling Museum*

Along Rhode Island's East Bay, in a stretch of perhaps 20 miles, a dozen companies carry on a tradition of fine boatbuilding that started before the American Revolution. From colonial days through the 1800s, Rhode Island craftsmen were famed for their merchant vessels, navy ships, and whalers. But it was the growth of a leisure class in the late 1800s that brought Rhode Island its true boating glory. It all started in 1893 when Vigilant, a racing yacht built by the Herreshoff brothers of Bristol, defeated Valkyrie II to win the America's Cup. The Herreshoffs went on to build five victorious America's Cup yachts. In the years since, dozens of Rhode Island companies have led the recreational boatbuilding industry, pioneering such innovations as fiberglass cruisers, new keel designs, and state-of-the-art navigation and communication devices. Although the America's Cup races left Rhode Island after America's 1983 loss to Australia, locally built yachts still dominate the competition. One Bristol firm has built nine America's Cup boats—including 1992 winner Stars and Stripes and all three U.S. contenders for the 1995 race. ◉

The boats built in Bristol today by craftsmen such as Eric Goetz, above, are much more high-tech than those built by the Herreshoff brothers 100 years ago. *Photo Billy Black. Left: Reliance,* built in 1903 by the Herreshoff Manufacturing Company of Bristol, was the largest America's Cup defender ever built. *Photo C. Bolles, Herreshoff Marine Museum*

Grade-school history lessons taught us that the Puritans sailed to the New World in search of religious freedom. True enough, but it turned out they had no interest in allowing others such freedom. On the other hand, the early Rhode Islanders meant it when they said their colony would be a safe haven for people of different faiths, and many came to share in the beneficence of that promise. Touro Synagogue, built in 1763, is North America's oldest synagogue. Quakers arriving in the mid-1600s built the country's first Quaker meeting house, in Newport, and were a powerful political force in colonial life. America's first Baptist Church was formed in Providence in 1639. That famous tolerance evaporated for a time in the late 19th and early 20th centuries, when waves of Roman Catholic Irish, French, and Italian immigrants found doors literally slammed in their faces when they looked for work and housing. But today, more than 60 percent of Rhode Islanders call themselves Roman Catholics. ◉

> *". . . a Government which gives to bigotry no sanction, to persecution no assistance . . ."*
>
> George Washington, in a 1790 letter to the membership of Touro Synagogue.

Opposite: John Fitzgerald Kennedy and Jacqueline Bouvier exchanged wedding vows in September 1953 at St. Mary's Church, Newport. St. Mary's is the state's oldest Roman Catholic parish. *Corbis-Bettmann. Above:* A collection box used by the First Baptist Church of Westerly, c. 1835. *Museum of Art, Rhode Island School of Design. Left:* Touro Synagogue, built in Newport in 1763, was the first synagogue in America. *Newport Historical Society*

BRISTOL FERRY One Hundred years ago

BRISTOL

The Short Line
between Newport and Providence
Bristol Ferry today

The Short Line

SAFETY   SERVICE   ECONOMY   COMFORT

LINES   LINES

Bridges to Progress

If water is Rhode Island's beauty, bridges are its accessories—glorious spans that do far more than simply connect point to point. The Claiborne Pell Bridge, joining Newport and Jamestown, is New England's longest suspension bridge. Second-longest is the pretty Mount Hope Bridge, built in 1929 to link northern Aquidneck Island to the mainland. Along with the Sakonnet and Jamestown–Verrazzano bridges, these spans changed the nature of the state, turning out-of-the-way island towns into accessible communities. Beyond making commuters' lives easier, the bridges offer a daily reminder of the state's beauty. From any bridge, you can see at least one other stretching

The Mount Hope Bridge, completed in 1929, replaced the ferry service that had operated since 1698 between Aquidneck Island and Bristol. *Newport Historical Society*

across the sparkling bay, and from the Jamestown–Verrazzano on a clear day you can see Block Island to the south and the Providence skyline to the north. Inland, in Foster, sits the shortest covered bridge in New England. And in the middle of the river between Providence and East Providence stands the curious "stuck-up" bridge, a rusted old railroad drawbridge that no one now living has ever seen closed.

Workmen in this 1929 photo string cable along the Mount Hope Bridge's center span. *Photo Avery Lord, courtesy Rhode Island Historical Society. Below:* The Newport Bridge was completed in 1969, linking Aquidneck Island at its southern tip in Newport to Jamestown. *Photo Jim Schwabel/New England Stock Photo*

"WE RODE HOME ON THE BOW OF MY FATHER'S SAILBOAT, THE WATER all sunset colors until the sun was gone. Then the water turned black and we pulled our trailing feet from the waves. By the time we reached home it was dark. Newport glowed pink on the horizon. The Newport Bridge was a necklace of lights nudging the sky."

Paul Watkins, Stand Before Your God, *1993*

Block Island's Southeast Light was saved from doom in 1993 when it was moved 200 feet back from the bluff on which it stands. *Photo Malcolm Greenaway.* **Below:** The light at Point Judith, in Narragansett, guards Rhode Island Sound. *Photo Thomas H. Mitchell/New England Stock Photo.* **Opposite top:** Lisa Nolan, keeper of the Southeast Light, Block Island. *Photo Kelly-Mooney Photography/ Corbis.* **Opposite bottom:** The Block Island ferry passes by Newport's Castle Hill Light. *Photo Thomas Mitchell/New England Stock Photo*

Shining Pride

Rhode Islanders are justifiably proud of the 21 lighthouses that testify to the state's past glory in the merchant trade and present status as a sailor's paradise. At the nation's third-oldest lighthouse, Beavertail Light, built in 1749 on Jamestown's northernmost post, scores of volunteers run nature programs and staff a museum. Off Newport, Rose Island's renovated lighthouse is now a bed and breakfast, where visitors help maintain the house and grounds as part of their payment. Hundreds of citizens rallied in 1993 to raise the money to move Block Island's Southeast Light some 200 feet back from its precarious perch on a

cliff above the ocean, ensuring its role as protector of sailors for generations. Although only 13 lights still shine, all are cherished by the state's residents, and many are in various stages of rebirth.

"THE LIGHT IS MY CHILD, AND I KNOW WHEN IT NEEDS me, even if I sleep."

Ida Lewis, who lived at Limerock Lighthouse from 1854 to 1911

Lady of the House

Lighthouse-keeping was mostly man's work, but no man ever outshone Ida Lewis in bravery. Ida's father became the lighthouse keeper at Newport's Limerock Light in 1854; when he fell ill three years later, his wife and 19-year-old Ida took over. Limerock was near a busy port, and Ida often had to row out into stormy waters to rescue foolish schoolboys, drunken sailors, and once, a boatful of sheep. Word of her feats spread, *Harper's Weekly* wrote her up, and Ida became a national hero, much to her embarrassment. She tended the light until her death in 1911. Visitors can see Ida's rowboat at the Newport Historical Society and visit her grave overlooking Newport Harbor.

The quadrangle at Brown University. *Photo Michael Dwyer/Stock Boston. Below:* The entrance to Johnson & Wales new downtown Providence campus. *Courtesy Johnson & Wales*

The smallest state has some big names in education. The nationally renowned Rhode Island School of Design, founded in 1877 by a group of Providence matrons, is the alma mater of countless successful artists. Since 1884, the Naval War College at Newport has been the Navy's primary education center. The Ivy League Brown University opened in 1764, and in 1790 granted George Washington an honorary Doctor of Laws degree. The University of Rhode Island, established in 1892 as a land grant agriculture school, today has one of the nation's best graduate schools

of oceanography. At the university's Narragansett Bay campus, some 200 research programs, accounting for $21 million in federal funds, study subjects ranging from the dynamics of ocean circulation to how whales and dolphins communicate. Johnson and Wales opened as a business school in 1914 with two typewriters and one student. Today it has the largest culinary arts and hospitality program in the world, with campuses in five states and study opportunities in several countries.

The Really Old School

Emperor Constantine the Great would surely be surprised to know that the university he founded in 330 A.D.—the oldest in the world—is now based in Rhode Island. By the early 20th century, the university had lost the financial support of the Italian government. But the Italian prince who headed the institution persuaded a Rhode Islander he'd met during World War II to take it over. Today Constantinian University is run largely out of a file cabinet but retains its charter and holds scholarly seminars, as well as an annual convocation at which honorary degrees are awarded to international luminaries.

A poster commemorates the 1916 Tournament of Roses football game between Brown University and the State College of Washington. *Brown University, Special Collections*

Capital Improvements

People gather on summer evenings for concerts at Waterplace Park, at the head of the river walk in downtown Providence. *Photo William H. Ewen, Jr.*

Since the mid-1980s, Providence has been transformed step by step from the gritty little city the *Wall Street Journal* called "a smudge on the highway to Cape Cod," to one of *Newsweek*'s Top Ten Cities. The first—and biggest—step took place with the rerouting of the sluggish Woonasquatucket and Moshassuck Rivers to make room for an attractive new downtown. Now the rivers flow easily under pretty footbridges and through Waterplace Park, where art festivals, concerts, and gondola rides keep lively crowds in the city beyond office hours. The 1990s saw the building of a convention center and luxury hotel,

Highlights of the Banner Trail

First Baptist Church
401-421-1177

Providence Athenaeum
401-421-7970

Governor Stephen
Hopkins House
401-884-8337

The Arcade
410-598-1199

Roger Williams
National Memorial
401-521-7266

Rhode Island
State House
401-222-2357

as well as Providence Place, a shopping center complete with a Nordstrom. Preservationists and artists have gotten in on the act, creating the Banner Trail, a series of colorful flags that lead visitors to Providence's many historic sites, galleries, and museums.

Downtown Providence's renaissance includes the river walk that runs along the foot of the city's historic East Side. *Photo William H. Ewen, Jr. Above: Postcard of Providence. Lake County Museum/Corbis*

John O. Pastore, Rhode Island's first Italian-American governor and senator, delivered the keynote speech at the 1964 Democratic National Convention. *Providence College Archives*

Beginning with its founding, Rhode Island's independent spirit raised eyebrows outside its borders. To the individualist, Roger Williams's colony was a haven; to the conformist it was a moral sewer. After the Revolutionary War, Rhode Island was a laughingstock and a pariah as its legislature voted 13 times not to ratify the Constitution before finally acquiescing in 1790. Through the late 19th century, state politics were controlled by a powerful clique of well-born Republican Yankees, but as the century turned, power shifted dramatically toward the working class as the mostly Irish-controlled Democrats gained sway. In 1906 James Higgins became the state's first Irish Catholic governor. The tolerance that characterized the founding of the state lives on in its political life. Rhode Island is mostly a state of Democrats with liberal social leanings. Though 60 percent of its citizens are Roman Catholic, Rhode Islanders prefer to let people fight their own moral battles, consistently voting, for example, against legislation to ban abortion. Still, never a people to avoid contradiction, when

The re-lighting of Block Island's Southeast Light, in August 1994, was cause for celebration. Attending the ceremony were, left to right: Marjorie and Governor Bruce Sundlun, Senators John Chafee and Claiborne Pell, and Congressman (now Senator) Jack Reed. *Photo Malcolm Greenaway*

Rhode Islanders find a Republican they like, they're loyal. Senator John H. Chafee was a three-term governor and served as U.S. senator from 1976 until his death in 1999. ◉

HAIL, REALM OF ROGUES, RENOWNED FOR FRAUD AND GUILE,
All hail, the knaveries of yon little isle. . . .
Look through the state, the unhallowed ground appears
A nest of dragons and a cave for bears. . . .
The wiser race, the snare of law to shun,
Like Lot from Sodom, from Rhode Island run.

*From a 1787 Connecticut newspaper, about
Rhode Island's refusal to ratify the U.S. Constitution*

The Brown House, on Providence's East Side, is among the finest existing examples of Federal period architecture. *Photo G. E. Kidder Smith/Corbis*

Saints Preserved Them

Of all the states, Rhode Island has the highest percentage of buildings on the National Register of Historic Places, thanks to efforts that began in 1945, when the Newport Preservation Society formed to restore Hunter House, the grand 1738 home of a prosperous merchant. The Newport Restoration Foundation, created by tobacco heiress Doris Duke in the 1960s, has salvaged more than 100 of the city's precious stash of 18th- and 19th-century Colonial and Federal houses. The centerpiece for preservation, though, is Providence's Benefit Street, which embodies the colonists' strong belief in the separation of church and state. Where other colonies built town greens anchored by a church, Providence chose a more egalitarian layout, with merchants' mansions and craftsmen's houses side by side along the waterfront. On and near Benefit Street— the "Mile of History"—stand some of the country's most magnificent early houses, including the John Brown house, built in the 1780s by a merchant who amassed a fortune in the China trade. President John Quincy Adams called the three-story Federal house "the most magnificent and elegant private mansion I have ever seen on this continent."

Beautifully restored Colonial houses line Benefit Street, Providence's "Mile of History." Photo Jim Schwabel/New England Stock Photo

The Elms, built from 1899–1902 as the Newport summer "cottage" of coal magnate Edward Julius Berwind, was designed by Horace Trumbauer, a Philadelphia architect who modeled the house after the Château d'Agnès at Asnières, France. *Courtesy of the Preservation Society of Newport County. Below:* The Gold Ballroom of the Marble House, built in 1888–92 by Richard Morris Hunt for William K. Vanderbilt, set the standard for opulence among Newport's wealthy. *Photo Farrell Grehan/Photo Researchers, Inc.*

A Summer Place

The late-19th-century industrialists of New York, Philadelphia, and South Carolina loved to flaunt their riches, and Newport made a perfect showcase. With its cooling ocean breezes, soothing vistas, and a reputation for wealth and culture dating from colonial days, it became a stylish summer retreat for Vanderbilts, Belmonts, and Astors, who built mansions one after another, each more opulent than the last, along Bellevue Avenue and the Cliff Walk. Under the scrutiny of Mrs. Caro-

line Astor and self-styled arbiter of taste Ward McAllister, the social elite gathered for all-night soirees in the grand ballrooms of the Breakers, Marble House, and other "cottages," designed by such architectural luminaries as Richard Morris Hunt and Stanford White to replicate European palaces. Less ostentatious, if no less wealthy, families spent time in Newport, too. Jacqueline Bouvier summered at Hammersmith Farm, the home of her stepfather, Hugh D. Auchincloss, as a teenager and later with her husband, President John F. Kennedy. President Dwight D. Eisenhower and his wife chose a "summer White House" in Newport in the 1950s; the Victorian mansion overlooking Newport Harbor was later renamed Eisenhower House.

The Breakers, Cornelius Vanderbilt's home on Ochre Point, overlooking the Cliff Walk and the ocean, may be the most famous of the opulent Newport mansions. *Photo Mathias Oppersdorff/ Photo Researchers, Inc.*

"NEWPORT WAS NOW AT ITS BEST. THE MOST CHARMING PEOPLE OF the country had formed a select little community there; the society was small and all were included in the gaieties and festivities. Those were the days that made Newport what it was then and is now—the most enjoyable and luxurious little island in America."

Ward McAllister, in his memoir, Society As I have Found It

Animals, birds, and other topiaries populate the Green Animals Topiary Gardens, in Portsmouth. *Photo Jim Schwabel/New England Stock Photo. Opposite:* Rare species of plants and trees are among thousands of plants and flowers at Blithewold Mansion, in Bristol. *Photo Craig Blouin/New England Stock Photo*

Glorious Gardens

One expects fine homes to have beautiful gardens, and Rhode Island's don't disappoint. Visitors come to Blithewold, a 33-acre Victorian-era estate on the bay in Bristol, primarily for the spectacular display of thousands of daffodils each spring, but the garden also boasts the largest redwood tree east of the Rockies. At the Elms, one of the famous Newport cottages, not a single elm tree remains, but the classical gardens planted between 1907 and 1914 still enchant with mazelike hedges, marble and bronze sculptures and fountains, and formal sunken flower gardens. Nowhere is a garden more lovingly tended, and more delightful, than at Green Animals, a Victorian country estate in Portsmouth. Here, 80 ornamental topiaries—including 21 in the shapes of animals and birds—stand watch over seven acres along Narragansett Bay. Joseph Carreiro cared for the topiaries from 1905 to 1945, then turned his shears over to his son-in-law, George Mendonça, who retired in 1985. The Preservation Society of Newport County now maintains the gardens, which are open to the public.

Earthly Edens

A sampling of gardens worth a special trip.

Blithewold Mansion and Gardens
Bristol, 401-253-2707
33 acres of gardens; many rare and unusual specimens

The Elms
Newport, 401-847-1000
Classical plantings with formal hedges and bronze sculptures

Green Animals
Portsmouth, 401-847-1000
Elaborate topiaries

Theatre-by-the-Sea
Matunuck, 401-782-3644
Stunning three-season garden is the setting for summer stock theater

The Arboretum at Wilcox Park
Westerly, 401-596-8590
Designed by a descendent of Frederick Law Olmsted

A Chippendale mahogany block-front and shell-carved chest from the Townsend-Goddard workshops, Newport c. 1750–60. *Christie's Images. Below:* Among the treasures at Newport's Whitehorne House, a Federal period house open for tours, is a mahogany block-and-shell chest-on-chest attributed to the Townsend-Goddard furniture makers. *Newport Historical Society Opposite:* A maple Queen Ann chest made in Rhode Island, c. 1740–60. *Christie's Images*

Crafting a Legacy

Throughout the colonies handcrafted furniture was prized, and no one created finer pieces than the Townsend and the Goddard families of Newport. Three generations of Townsends and Goddards worked together, beginning in the mid-1700s, crafting as many as 10,000 pieces of furniture—pieces that experts today call the finest furniture of the period. In 1999, a circa 1745 slant-top desk made by Christopher Townsend sold for $8.25 million at Sotheby's. The only piece of American furniture that ever brought more money was a 1767 desk made by John Goddard, which went for $12.1 million at Christie's in 1989. Today, Rhode Island is still noted for its abundance of fine furniture makers, many of whom studied at the Rhode Island School of Design. Some make replicas of colonial furniture, complete with dovetail joints, whereas others have earned national reputations for work that may look more modern in design but whose quality pays homage to the techniques of those early artisans.

This mahogany, pine, and ivory tall case clock was made in Providence in 1816. *Museum of Art, Rhode Island School of Design*

Sailing regattas are a common sight in the waters off Newport. *Photo Malcolm Greenaway. Below:* Preparation for the America's Cup. *Corbis. Opposite bottom:* Flag-festooned yachts at Newport's docks celebrate the New York Yacht Club's 150th anniversary, in 1996. *Photo Onne Van Der Wal/Stock Newport*

For more than 50 years, sailors competed off Newport for the America's Cup. The races left Newport when Australia won the cup in 1983—a temporary condition, Rhode Islanders hope—but Narragansett Bay is still a sailor's heaven. A number of Olympic and America's Cup contenders live and train in Rhode Island, and Newport still hosts important sailing races, including the Around the World solo competition and the Newport to Bermuda race. The hundreds of recreational sailboats and powerboats that dot the bay on all but the coldest days attest to Rhode Islanders' fondness for matching their wits with the wind and waves. ◉

"Narragansett Bay"

The sales are all unfurled, the streamers proud
Sport in the breeze, and gay as childhood now
We skim the silver wave, which sparkles round our prow.
Majestic Narragansett, o'er whose breast
Our barque is lightly wafted by the breeze,
Fondly encircled, on thy bosom rest
The nursing isles.

James D. Knowles, 1841, from
Rhode Island in Verse, *1936*

Newport's high society
takes in the exciting
scene at a New York
Yacht Club Race in Cas-
tle Hill, 1885. *Newport
Historical Society*

The Sporting Life

Those who prefer to recreate on dry land rather than the briny deep can get their fill of tennis, golf, and polo in Rhode Island. Newport's Tennis Casino hosts both the International Tennis Hall of Fame and the only grass-court tournaments in the country. The Newport Country Club is the country's second-oldest private golf course. Portsmouth's Polo Grounds have earned a reputation for world-class polo tournaments.

Not all of Rhode Island's sports are so genteel, however. Skateboarders plunged down the steep hills of Providence and bungee jumpers threw themselves off towers when the state hosted the first ESPN X Games in 1997 and 1998 and the first Gravity Games in 1999. And although the state is hardly known for its mountains, the collection of boulders in the park at Lincoln Woods, just north of Providence, is regarded as a top-notch place for rock climbing.

Croquet players play on the grounds of an estate on Newport's Bellevue Avenue, 1983. *Photo Patrick Ward/ Corbis*

The Casino, home of the International Tennis Hall of Fame, is one of America's oldest country clubs, built in Newport in 1879–81 by McKim, Mead and White. *Photo Onne Van Der Wal/Stock Newport Below:* Tennis at Newport Casino, c. 1885. *Newport Historical Society*

St. Patrick's Day parade in Newport. *Photo Billy Black.* Opposite top: Clowns in Block Island's 4th of July parade. *Photo Malcolm Greenaway.* Opposite bottom: The Bristol 4th of July parade is the oldest in the nation. *Rhode Island Tourism Division*

Something to Celebrate

Rhode Islanders love a celebration. The first Labor Day parade was reportedly held in Rhode Island, in 1882. In Bristol, the lines down the center of the streets are permanently painted red, white, and blue to mark the route of the nation's oldest Fourth of July parade—first held in 1786—and real estate ads tout "on the parade route" as a selling point. Nearly every ethnic group holds an annual parade and "feast" with carnival rides, booths, and foods. The granddaddy of such events is the Italian festival held Columbus Day weekend on Providence's Federal Hill. People swarm the streets—with lines painted red and green for the occasion—to watch the parade, listen to music, catch up with friends, and eat sausage and pepper sandwiches and doughboys. Quieter but no less festive is Rhode Island's unique way of welcoming spring. On May 1, in church halls and community centers all over the state, people gather for May breakfasts—bacon, egg, and jonnycake orgies—to welcome the season.

Favorite Fests

A handful of not-to-be-missed festivals.

Gaspee Days Commemorates the 1769 burning of the British sloop *Gaspee;* May

Black Ships Festival Celebrates Commodore Perry's 1853 mission to open trade with Japan; July

International Quahog Festival Honors Rhode Island's favorite food; August

Columbus Day Festival Highlights Providence's Italian heritage; October

A trio of friends out for a walk and a dip at the beach at Narragansett in 1913. *Culver Pictures*

Rhode Island may be short on land, but it's long on shoreline, and residents take full advantage of the hundred or so public and private beaches scattered along the state's meandering coast. The beauty of the state's beaches is that they remain pristine and undeveloped. No high-rise condominiums or waterfront shopping centers hide the view of the ocean or prevent beach-goers from making their way to the sandy shore. Instead, salt-washed, sun-bleached shingled cottages house little colonies of summer folks—many of whom live in Warwick or Providence, just 20 or so miles away, but keep these second houses to make the most of short summers and long stretches of beach. While many are content to lie on the sand and frolic in the waves, die-hard surfers battle the waves at Newport's beaches all year long. Divers know that several Rhode Island spots, including the rocky point off Fort Whetherill in Jamestown, are treasure troves for exploring unusual sea life.

WHETHER THE SUMMER WAVES SERENELY SMILE,
Or wintry breakers dash with solemn roar
Around thy stern and wild—thy noble shore—
Thou has a charm no pen or tongue can tell.

Charles T. Brooks, 1841, from Rhode Island in Verse, *1936*

Miles of pristine beaches, like this one at Watch Hill (at left and above), in Westerly, stretch along Rhode Island's southern shore. *Photo Jim Schwabel/New England Stock Photo*

Newport's Redwood Library, built in 1748, is the country's third-oldest private library— and the oldest still housed in its original building. *Photo Allison Langley/ Stock Newport. Below:* The grandson of artist John La Farge, Oliver Hazard Perry La Farge won the 1929 Pulitzer Prize for fiction for his novel *Laughing Boy. Culver Pictures*

A Writers' Refuge

Rhode Island claims only a handful of native-born big-name writers, but it has a long reputation for inspiring literary greatness. One of the state's few native sons, the horror writer H. P. Lovecraft—today a cult figure for lovers of the macabre— died alone and destitute in Providence in 1937, convinced of his own failure. Thankfully, many writers who spent time in the state achieved greater acclaim in their lifetimes. Edgar Allan Poe came to Providence to write and left with a broken heart after an unrequited romance. Bostonians Henry James and Edith Wharton summered in Newport, and several of James's books, including his final, unfinished novel, *The Ivory Tower,* revolve around Newport society. Another sometime New-porter, Maud Howe Elliott, won the Pulitzer Prize for her 1917

biography of her mother, Julia Ward Howe, the composer of "The Battle Hymn of the Republic." Oliver La Farge—full name Oliver Hazard Perry La Farge and grandson of the artist John La Farge—took the fiction prize in 1929. Thornton Wilder, stationed in Newport during World War I, returned later to write *Theophilus North*, set in that city. The humorist S. J. Perelman grew up in Providence, and Cormac McCarthy, whose *Border Trilogy* novels have been much acclaimed, was born in the capital.

Thornton Wilder set his novel *Theophilus North* in Newport. *Culver Pictures*

"I AM ALWAYS LOOKING AT THE HARBOR AND SOMEDAY I WANT to be buried beside it, at the foot of Walley Street, in the brilliant green grass that precedes the drop to a small shingle. There I'll be toe to toe with Indian bones, and gazing out at Poppasquash."

Mary Cantwell, from her memoir American Girl, 1992

Kiddie Literature

Two of today's foremost illustrator/authors call Rhode Island home. Chris Van Allsburg, a Caldecott Medal winner, wrote and illustrated the popular *Polar Express,* as well as *Jumanji,* which became a movie. David A. Macaulay is perhaps best known for his *The Way Things Work* books with their precise architectural drawings and fascinating, easy-to-grasp explanations for how all manner of machines operate.

Rhode Island on Stage and Screen

A scene from Trinity Rep's production of *A Christmas Carol*. Photo T. Charles Erickson. Right: Playwright Paula Vogel won the Pulitzer Prize for *How I Learned to Drive*. Photofest. Opposite: Filmmakers Bobby Farrelly and Peter Farrelly with Cameron Diaz on the set of *There's Something About Mary*, 1998. *Photofest*

Rhode Island's lively theater scene embraces dozens of small theaters presenting everything from the avant-garde to the time-honored. The summer stock productions of Matunuck's Theatre-by-the-Sea have won national recognition. Presiding above all is Trinity Repertory Company, a 1982 Tony Award winner considered among America's best regional companies. Its resident set designer, Eugene Lee, designed the sets for *Saturday Night Live* from 1974 to

1980 and won Tony Awards for Broadway productions of *Candide* and *Sweeney Todd*. Tim Daly, co-star of the long-running television series *Wings*, got his start at Trinity Rep. Rhode Islanders have found success beyond Trinity, too. Playwright Paula Vogel won the 1998 Pulitzer Prize for her Broadway hit *How I Learned to Drive*. Movie star James Woods grew up in Rhode Island, as did the late actor J. T. Walsh, who played John Erlichman to Woods's H. R. Haldeman in Oliver Stone's 1995 movie *Nixon*. Nowadays, the popular TV drama *Providence* beams images of the capital to screens across the land and draws tourists to see it first-hand.

Reel-Life Rhode Island

A handful of large- and small-screen productions filmed at least partly in the state.

The Great Gatsby Newport's Rosecliff mansion hosts the lavish parties and high drama of the F. Scott Fitzgerald novel; 1974

Mr. North Based on *Theophilus North*, the Thornton Wilder novel set in Rhode Island, starring Angelica Huston and Lauren Bacall; 1988

Dumb and Dumber Buddy comedy with Jim Carrey and Jeff Daniels, written by Rhode Island brothers Bobby and Peter Farrelly; 1994

True Lies Mega-action flick with Arnold Schwarzenegger and scenes at Newport's Ochre Court mansion; 1994

Federal Hill Young Italian-American men learn about loyalty to friends and "the family," starring John Turturro, directed by Rhode Islander Michael Corrente; 1995

Amistad Newport stood in for colonial New Haven in Steven Spielberg's antislavery epic; 1997

Fast, Cheap & Out of Control Errol Morris's documentary features George Mendoça, the retired topiary gardener of Green Animals; 1997

Meet Joe Black Brad Pitt as the devil spars with Anthony Hopkins; filmed at Aldrich Mansion, Warwick; 1998

There's Something About Mary Screwball comedy starring Ben Stiller and Cameron Diaz, written by the Farrelly brothers; 1998

James Cagney starred as George M. Cohan in the 1942 bio-pic *Yankee Doodle Dandy. Photofest*

Biographers dispute George M. Cohan's birthday—he claimed July 4, 1878, although some say he fudged the actual date of July 3—but no one argues that he was among the most popular of all vaudeville entertainers. Born in Providence to a family of performers, Cohan was on the road singing and dancing by the time he reached his teens. (His family left Rhode Island as the boy was entering his teens, but the state still claims him as its

LIFE IS WHAT YOU MAKE IT, IT'S JUST THE WAY YOU TAKE IT,
Life can be a tragedy or life can be a song.
Scientific teachers, philosophers and preachers
Have forty different themes on the way to get along.
But when all is said and done, why do they worry so?
To me to look on life is just like looking at a show.

Lyrics from "Life Is Like a Musical Comedy,"
a song in George M. Cohan's last (and autobiographical) musical,
The Musical Comedy Man, *1941*

own.) Although his entire formal education
consisted of six weeks at a Providence elementary
school when he was seven, he turned into a pro-

lific writer, penning as many
as 500 songs and 80 plays.
Critics thought little of his
playwriting talents, but
Cohan is the undisputed
king of patriotic songs,
including "Yankee Doodle
Boy," "Grand Old Flag," and
"Over There"—anthems
that aroused the nationalis-
tic passion of American sol-
diers fighting in the two
World Wars. ◉

Sheet music for "Over
There," a patriotic war
song penned by Cohan.
LPW, Inc. Left: Provi-
dence native George M.
Cohan wrote scores of
plays and hundreds of
songs, including the
patriotic hits "Yankee
Doodle Dandy" and
"Over There." *Culver
Pictures*

The Newport Folk Festival, 1989. Four decades after its founding, the event still draws crowds to Fort Adams State Park. *Photo Richard Pasley/Stock Boston.* *Below:* Bob Dylan at the Newport Folk Festival, 1963. Dylan scandalized the folk music world two years later when he played an electric guitar at the festival. *Photo William H. Ewen, Jr.*

A Place for Music

Bob Dylan shocked the sensibilities of folkies when he fired up his electric guitar at the 1965 Newport Folk Festival. It was a fit-

ting place to cause a stir: Newport had been on music's cutting edge since the city hosted its first Jazz Festival in 1953. The Newport Folk Festival was born in 1959. Locals weren't always happy with the boisterous outlander hordes who came to hear the music, and a series of riots in the late sixties ended the festivals temporarily. Now, both jazz and folk festivals have returned, playing to audiences less rowdy but no less ardent. They've been joined by the Newport Music Festival, a series of orchestral and chamber performances in the town's gilded mansions—a great place to witness the debuts of talented young performers. Rhode Island's colleges and clubs have nurtured some terrific home-grown talent: contemporary headliners who got their start here include the rock groups Talking Heads and Throwing Muses and pop singer Jeffrey Osborne.

Pop singer Jeffrey Osborne maintains strong ties to his large, close-knit Rhode Island family. *Photofest.* **Left: One-time Rhode Islander David Byrne, of Talking Heads fame, in the concert film** *Stop Making Sense,* **1984.** *Photofest*

Pastoral Study, Paradise, Rhode Island by John La Farge, c. 1864. *Yale University Art Gallery, New Haven. Right: Peacocks and Peonies II* by John La Farge, 1882. La Farge invented opalescent stained glass in 1879, for which he received the Légion d'honneur in 1889. He soon had many imitators, including Louis Comfort Tiffany. *National Museum of American Art, Washington, D.C./Art Resource, NY*

It's impossible to exaggerate Narragansett Bay's importance to Rhode Island, from its days as a colonial trading center to its present status as a vacation destination. Its role in art is no exception. The bay—especially in and near Newport—figured significantly in the history of American art. Just as the area drew intellectuals and writers of the 18th and 19th centuries, so it lured masters of the American Impressionist, Hudson River, and other important schools to paint its serene landscapes. John Frederick Kensett, John La Farge, William Trost Richards, Daniel Huntington, and others took inspiration from the rocky shores, pastoral scenes, and unusual light of South County and Aquidneck Island. Newport's wealth brought portrait artists to the city as well. Colonial portraitists John Smibert and Joseph Blackburn and,

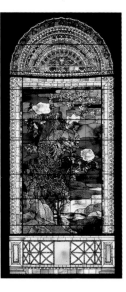

Newport, Rhode Island by William Trost Richards, c. 1880. Richards produced dozens of seascapes of Newport and Rhode Island's shoreline. From the 1870s until his death in 1905, he spent part of every year in the Newport area. *Photo Ted Hendrickson. Private collection. Below:* A painted panel box by Sydney Burleigh, a leader of the Arts and Crafts movement in 19th-century Rhode Island. *Museum of Art, Rhode Island School of Design*

later, John Singer Sargent found eager patrons among the successful merchants and their families. The presence of these artists engendered the founding of the Rhode Island School of Design and the venerable Providence Art Club and brought a vitality to the local art scene that continues to flourish. ◉

"THE CHARM OF SOLITUDE IS GONE FOREVER, but the beauty of detail still remains, and nothing can destroy the deep satisfaction we have in our own little Kingdom and the wide sea."

> *From a late 19th-century letter by William Trost Richards to a friend, about Jamestown's increasing popularity as a resort*

The RISD Connection

Providence claims to have more artists per capita than any other American city. Given that one of the country's finest art schools, the Rhode Island School of Design, is located here, it might well be true. RISD-trained artists contribute enormously to the state's cultural landscape, even before graduation. Hundreds of locals attend the annual RISD fashion show to view student designs from the beautifully wearable to . . . well, how would one describe an ensemble made of neon-orange traffic cones? Many of RISD's fashion grads go on to work at top design houses or—like Nicole Miller, known for her vivid, whimsical designs for men and women—start their own companies. No Rhode Island woman needs to wear factory-made jewelry when hand-crafted pieces by scores of RISD-trained metalsmiths are offered in boutiques from Westerly to Providence. And the RISD museum, one of the nation's finest small museums, exhibits art from Egyptian antiquities to contemporary fine art by local artists.

A Short List of RISD Graduates

Richard Byrne, icono-clastic pop musician; attended in early 1970s (he never graduated)

Roz Chast, cartoonist most noted for her *New Yorker* drawings; 1977

David Macauley, illustrator and author of *The Way Things Work, Cathedral,* and other books; 1969

Richard Merkin, painter and writer for *The New Yorker, GQ, Vanity Fair,* and *Harper's;* 1963

Nicole Miller, fashion designer; 1973

Martin Mull, painter, comedian, and actor; 1965

Falling/Rising Man by Craig Kraft, 1998, was part of Convergence XI, Rhode Island's statewide public arts festival. *Photo by Craig Kraft/ Courtesy Providence Parks Department*

In the Public Eye

There's a special delight in happening on a work of art in an unexpected place—a fanciful sculpture at a busy intersection, say, or a mural on a downtown building. Rhode Island's abundance of public art provides plenty of those eye-opening encounters. Providence's pride and joy is *WaterFire,* the brainchild of RISD graduate Barnaby Evans, who conceived the idea of lighting a series of fires in cauldrons on the rivers that run through the city. On warm nights people flock by the thousands to watch the fires and listen to the music that wafts downriver on the evening breeze. And who but RISD students would think up *PumpkinFire*—a respectful send-up of *WaterFire* in which elaborately carved jack o' lanterns are displayed in conjunction with the show. Convergence, a ten-day statewide festival of public performances and installations by artists, is fast earning a reputation outside Rhode Island's borders. From the trompe l'oeil of a peeling facade on a Providence office building to a whimsical statue of feet sticking up out of a wave on Newport's Thames Street, the unexpected is an everyday thing in Rhode Island.

WaterFire **was the creation of a RISD graduate.** *Photo Billy Black*

Contemporary Stars

Countless artists seem to find their muse in the Ocean State, and Rhode Islanders cherish them in return. Even those who made a name here and then moved on, such as the preeminent glass artist Dale Chihuly, are still counted as Rhode Islanders by locals. Many renowned contemporary artists still call the state home, however, and no one genre or medium describes the state's vital arts scene. Howard Ben Tré's glass fountains and other sculptures have been installed in plazas, parks, and corporate offices all over the country and featured in museums worldwide. African-American painter Joe Norman's work was celebrated in a retrospective at the Boston Museum of Fine Arts before he was 40 years old. The enigmatic cut-paper silhouettes of Kara Walker have made her one of the country's hottest young artists. And metalsmith Jonathan Bonner's weathervanes and other sculptures have found their way into public and private collections nationwide.

Kay Ritter with some of her papier-mâché creations, 1990. *Photo Bob Rowan, Progressive Image/Corbis*

Foodies' Paradise

Martin Scorsese needed to know how an 1870s high-society table should be set. Julia Child wanted a recipe for Vermont oyster crackers. Whom did they ask? The folks at the Johnson and Wales Culinary Archives and Museum, of course. The Providence museum has the world's largest collection of culinary ephemera—more than 300,000 items, including 16th-century cookbooks, an 1874 stove, a bread ring buried in Pompeii when Vesuvius erupted, and a fourth-century Roman fish hook.

Midnight Snack

The diner originated in Providence in 1872, when Walter Scott sold food from a horse-drawn wagon to downtown workers on the late shift. Haven Brothers, one of the country's first sit-down diners, opened in 1893. Today's Haven Brothers is a converted 1950s truck, but its philosophy—good food, cheap—hasn't changed a whit in more than a century. It's Providence's great equalizer: on any night you'll rub elbows with theatergoers, bikers, even the mayor.

One Potato, Two Potato

When he was born in 1952, Mr. Potato Head was just a box of facial features and clothing; kids supplied their own potatoes. But when the Hasbro company found that kids would grab any vegetable handy, the toy maker wisely added a plastic potato to the kit. Maybe because it was the first toy ever advertised on TV, Mr. Potato Head became a star, selling, at last count, more than 50 million.

The Loved Bug

The Big Blue Bug, a two-ton steel and fiber-glass termite, first appeared on top of the New England Pest Control office building along Route 95 in Providence in 1980. Locals soon adopted him as an unofficial mascot, naming him Nibbles Woodaway in a 1990 statewide contest. Nibbles's fame crested in 1998 when he showed up in the movie *There's Something About Mary*.

Power House

Newport had plenty of taverns when William Mayes opened the White Horse Tavern in 1687, but his was a cut above, drawing influential landowners and lawmakers, the movers and shakers of the day. Today it's distinguished as the nation's oldest tavern building, having withstood wars, hurricanes, urban decay, even a stint as a house of ill repute in the early 20th century. Still a tavern and restaurant, it is again among the city's best.

Memory Lane

Brown and Hopkins Country Store, the nation's oldest continuously operating general store (built 1799), is still at the center of town life in Glocester. Customers stop in as much for the historic atmosphere as for the gourmet foodstuffs and handmade soaps and candles on sale. A roll-top desk has sat in the same spot since before the Civil War, and bygone products like laundry starch still dot the shelves. The penny candy costs more than a penny now, but the taste of nostalgia is worth it.

Great People

A selective listing of native and resident Rhode Islanders, concentrating on the arts.

Julia Ward Howe (1819–1910), descendent of two colonial governors, Newport summer resident, composer of "The Battle Hymn of the Republic"

Edward M. Bannister (1828–1901), one of a handful of important black painters of the 19th century

Alva Vanderbilt Belmont (1853–1933), socialite, supporter of the arts, mistress of Marble House, suffragist

Ruth Buzzi (b. 1936), actress, comedian, and regular on the 1960s TV show *Rowan and Martin's Laugh-in*

George M. Cohan (1878–1942), Providence-born actor, song-writer, producer, wrote "Give My Regards to Broadway," among hundreds of other tunes

Doris Duke (1913–1993), tobacco heiress who founded the Newport Restoration Foundation

Nelson Eddy (1901–1967), singer, movie star, and 1940s heartthrob

Eileen Farrell (b. 1920), Grammy-winning opera star

James Franklin (1697–1735), brother of Benjamin, established state's first printing press; founded the *Rhode Island Gazette*

John Goddard (1724–1785), first Goddard in the Townsend–Goddard families of fine furniture makers in Newport

Nathanael Greene Herreshoff (1848–1938), best-known of three brothers whose Bristol company built five winning America's Cup yachts

Van Johnson (b. 1916), actor, starred in 1954's *The Caine Mutiny*

Galway Kinnell (b. 1927), 1983 Pulitzer Prize–winning poet

John La Farge (1835–1910), painter and stained-glass artist, created mural and windows in the Newport Congregational Church

Oliver La Farge (1901–1963), novelist and summer visitor whose novel *Laughing Boy* won the Pulitzer Prize for fiction in 1929

Charles I. D. Looff (1852–1918), internationally noted carousel artisan

H. P. Lovecraft (1890–1937), Providence writer of macabre stories and short novels

S. J. Perelman (1904–1979) humorist, wrote scripts for the Marx Brothers movies *Horsefeathers* and *Monkey Business*; won an Oscar for his screenplay for *Around the World in Eighty Days*

Gilbert Stuart (1755–1828), North Kingstown–born painter most famous for his portrait of George Washington on $1 bill

John Townsend (1732–1804), one of the second generation of Townsend and Goddard furniture makers, often considered the group's best craftsman

. . . and Great Places

Some interesting derivations of Rhode Island place names.

Aquidneck Island Largest island in Rhode Island, from the Narragansett for "at the island."

Blackstone River Named for William Blackstone, the first European to settle in what became Rhode Island.

Block Island Named by the 17th-century Dutch explorer Adriaen Block.

Chariho Sounds like an Indian-derived name but is actually the familiar name of the combined towns of Charlestown, Richmond, and Hopkinton.

Charlestown Named for King Charles II, who granted Rhode Island its colonial charter.

Conanicut Island off Newport named after the Narragansett sachem who befriended Roger Williams. Translated, it means "at the especially long place."

Cowesett Neighborhood in Warwick, from the Narragansett for "place of young pine trees."

Federal Hill Also known as Little Italy, named for the grand homes built there during the Federal Period.

Frenchtown A section of East Greenwich settled by French Huguenots in 1686.

Jerusalem and Galilee Two villages in Narragansett, perhaps named because the bit of Narragansett Bay that divides them is so narrow one could almost walk across the water from one to the other.

Narragansett The bay and town took the name of the Indian nation that lived in Rhode Island, means "people of the small, narrow place."

Pocasset A section at the northern tip of Aquidneck, from the Narragansett for "where the stream widens."

Providence Named by Roger Williams, who was convinced that God's merciful providence led him to it.

Scalloptown A section of East Greenwich noted for its scallop beds in the early 20th century.

Slatersville Village named for Samuel Slater, the "father of American manufacturing."

Watch Hill A hilly point in the town of Westerly on Rhode Island Sound, named because its height afforded a great view of incoming enemy ships.

Benefit Street Providence's "Mile of History" with its many restored Colonial and Federal-style houses, named because its linear format (as opposed to a town square layout) was intended to benefit all neighborhood residents equally.

RHODE ISLAND BY THE SEASONS
A Perennial Calendar of Events and Festivals

Here is a selective listing of events that take place each year in the months noted; we suggest calling ahead to local tourism councils for dates and details.

January

Woonsocket
La Fete du Jour L'An
Traditional Canadian New Year's Day party.

February

Cranston
Cajun and Zydeco Mardi Gras Ball

Newport
Newport Winter Festival
Ten days of food, music, and other performances, and family activities.

Providence
Rhode Island Spring Flower and Garden Show

March

Newport
Irish Heritage Week
A week of Celtic music, dance, readings, and plays.
St. Patrick's Day Parade

April

Bristol
Daffodil Days
Blithewold Mansions, Garden and Arboretum display thousands of naturalized daffodils.

Providence
The Wheeler School Clothing Sale
State's highest-quality yard sale.

May

Statewide
May Breakfasts

Cranston
Gaspee Days
A festival commemorating the Colonial-era burning of the British sloop *Gaspee.*

Newport
Annual Used Boat Show
Scores of high-end sailboats and powerboats to ogle, along with races and other activities.
Nantucket Gold Regatta

Providence
RISD Fashion Show
Taste of the Nation
Tastings from Rhode Island restaurants, wineries, and breweries, to benefit hunger relief.
Women's Playwriting Festival

June

Newport
Newport International Film Festival
Two weeks of international films, classics, documentaries, and art films.

North Kingstown
Rhode Island National Guard Air Show
Air show featuring the Navy Leapfrogs, British Red Devils, and other aerial performers.

Providence
Convergence International Festival of the Arts
Ten days of performing arts, gallery tours, and public art installations.
Festival of Historic Houses
Tours of private period homes.

July

Bristol
Fourth of July Parade
Oldest in the nation.

Glocester
Ancient and Horribles Parade
An irreverent send-up of the past year's political events.

Newport
Black Ships Festival
A weekend of Japanese arts, foods, and performances.
Miller Lite Hall of Fame Tennis Championships
At the famous Newport Casino.
Newport Kite Festival
One-of-a-kind kites and competitions.

Newport Music Festival
Orchestral and chamber music performed in the famous mansions.

Wickford
Secret Garden Tours
Tours of tucked-away gardens of private homes in the historic village.

Wickford Art Festival
A juried festival featuring 250 national artists.

August

Barrington
CVS Charity Golf Classic
Pro golfers Brad Faxon and Billy Andrade lead a field of world-class golfers.

Block Island
Block Island Arts Festival

Charlestown
Charlestown Seafood Festival

Jamestown
Fool's Rules Regatta
Participants build boats on the shore using anything but marine materials, then race them.

Newport
JVC Jazz Festival
Newport Folk Festival

Providence
Best of Rhode Island Party
Annual party featuring winners of Rhode Island Monthly's "Best of Rhode Island" poll.

Richmond
Washington County Fair
A rural country fair with live-stock shows, country music, and a midway with rides.

Wickford
International Quahog Festival
A weekend of entertainment and family activities, with lots of foods made with quahogs.

September

Newport
Classic Yacht Regatta

Portsmouth
International Polo Series

Providence
Heritage Festival
A celebration of cultural diversity, on the State House lawn.

Warwick
Commicut Days Festival

October

Middletown
Norman Bird Sanctuary Harvest Fair

Newport
Oktoberfest
Waterfront Seafood Festival

Providence
Columbus Day Festival

Scituate
Scituate Art Festival

Woonsocket
Autumnfest Fall Festival

November

Providence
Fine Furnishings Show
Fine handcrafted furniture and home accessories by local and national artisans.

Ocean State Marathon

Warwick
Warwick Heritage Festival

December

Newport
Christmas in Newport
Concerts, candlelight tours, and door-decorating contests.

Opening Night
New Year's Eve celebration with performances and activities throughout the city.

Providence
A Christmas Carol
Trinity Repertory Company's annual production.

First Night New Year's Eve
Citywide alcohol-free celebration of the New Year.

RISD Alumni Holiday Sale
Fine arts and crafts by alumni of the renowned art school.

Wickford
Festival of Lights
Tree lighting, hayrides, entertainment, and a window-decorating contest.

WHERE TO GO
Museums, Attractions, Gardens, and Other Arts Resources

Call for seasons and hours when open.

Museums

DOLL MUSEUM
Thames St., Newport, 401-849-0405
Dolls from the early 18th century, doll houses, miniatures, and antique toys.

HAFFENREFFER MUSEUM OF ANTHROPOLOGY
Bristol, 401-253-8388
Artifacts from and exhibits about the Narragansett Bay region's Native Americans.

HERRESHOFF MARINE MUSEUM
Hope St., Bristol, 401-253-5000
Displays of sail and power yachts from the 1850s to the 1940s, plus the America's Cup hall of fame.

INTERNATIONAL TENNIS HALL OF FAME
Bellevue, Newport, 401-849-3990
Memorabilia, costumes, and exhibits about tennis through the years.

MUSEUM OF ART, RHODE ISLAND SCHOOL OF DESIGN
Providence, 401-454-6348
An impressive small museum with many fine collections from prehistory to the present.

MUSEUM OF YACHTING
Fort Adams, Newport, 401-847-1018
Exhibits on Newport's yachting past, plus a great view of Newport Harbor.

MUSEUM OF WORK AND CULTURE
Woonsocket, 401-769-9675
Exhibits about Rhode Island's ethnic groups and on the state's labor history.

NAVAL WAR COLLEGE MUSEUM
Coaster's Harbor Island, Newport, 401-848-8306
Exhibits and memorabilia from the history of the Navy, including a collection of World War II torpedoes.

NEWPORT ART MUSEUM
Bellevue Ave., Newport, 401-848-8200
Contemporary work as well as 18th- and 19th-century American masters.

PROVIDENCE CHILDREN'S MUSEUM
Providence, 401-273-5437
Interactive museum for children with exhibits on science, technology, cultural diversity, and more.

RHODE ISLAND FISHERMEN AND WHALE MUSEUM
Bowen's Wharf, Newport, 401-849-1340
Displays and interactive exhibits on the fishing and whaling industries.

RHODE ISLAND HOLOCAUST MEMORIAL MUSEUM
Kingston, 401-453-7860
Exhibits commemorating the Holocaust.

WILLIAM VAREIKA FINE ARTS
Bellevue Ave., Newport, 401-849-6149
A gallery and museum that features American masters of the 18th, 19th, and early 20th centuries, focusing on art of Narragansett Bay.

Attractions

BLACKSTONE VALLEY EXPLORER
Pawtucket, 401-724-1500
Narrated excursions on a 49-passenger river boat.

CLIFF WALK

A 3.5 mile stroll on a narrow walkway perched above the ocean, with backdoor views of Newport's mansions.

CRESCENT PARK CAROUSEL

Bullock's Point Rd., East Providence, 401-433-2828

Fully restored and operating carousel made by master craftsman Charles I. D. Looff in the 1890s.

FIRST BAPTIST CHURCH IN AMERICA

North Main St., Providence, 401-421-1177

The 1775 church has a 185-foot steeple and a massive 1792 Waterford crystal chandelier.

NATURE'S BEST DAIRY WORLD

Plainfield Pike, Cranston, 401-946-1122

Tours of a working dairy farm, with hands-on displays and an antique carousel.

NEWPORT AQUARIUM

Easton's Beach, Newport, 401-849-8430

An interactive museum with a touch tank for children.

NEWPORT ON FOOT GUIDED WALKING TOURS

Newport, 401-846-5391

Narrated walking tours of historic sites.

NORMAN BIRD SANCTUARY

Middletown, 401-846-2577

A 450-acre preserve overlooking the ocean.

OCEAN DRIVE

Starting at Bellevue Ave., Newport

A 10-mile drive that winds along the ocean past elegant 19th-century mansions.

PROVIDENCE ATHENAEUM

Benefit St., Providence, 401-421-6970

A 1753 library with rare book exhibits and rotating art shows.

PROVIDENCE PRESERVATION SOCIETY WALKING TOURS

Meeting St., Providence, 401-831-7440

Self-guided tours of the capital city's historic sites.

ROGER WILLIAMS PARK AND ZOO

Elmwood Ave., Providence, 401-785-9457 (park), 401-785-3520 (zoo)

A large park with museums, a carousel, a planetarium, and one of the country's best small zoos.

ROSE ISLAND LIGHT

Off Newport, 401-847-4242

Restored lighthouse and keeper's cottage where overnight visitors tend the light and do maintenance as part of their board.

SACHUEST POINT NATIONAL WILDLIFE REFUGE

Middletown, 401-364-9124

Salt marshes, grasslands, beaches, rocky cliffs, dunes, and hiking trails.

SAKONNET VINEYARDS

Main Rd., Little Compton, 401-635-8486

Tours and tastings year round.

SLATER MILL HISTORIC SITE

Roosevelt Ave., Pawtucket, 401-725-8638

America's first mechanized cotton mill, with exhibits, displays, and artifacts.

STATE HOUSE

Smith St., Providence, 401-222-2357

The McKim, Mead and White–designed state capitol sports the fourth-largest self-supported marble dome in the world, as well as fine art, murals, and historic documents.

TIVERTON FOUR CORNERS

Main Rd., Tiverton

A quaint intersection with antique shops and artisans, gourmet shops, and Gray's Ice Cream, a local institution.

TOURO SYNAGOGUE
Touro St., Newport, 401-847-4794
First Jewish house of worship in America.

TRINITY CHURCH
Queen Anne Sq., Newport, 401-846-0660
A 1726 Anglican church with an unusual three-tiered wineglass pulpit.

WATSON FARM
North Main Rd., Jamestown, 401-423-0005
Self-guided tours of a centuries-old working farm that sweeps down to the bay.

Homes and Gardens

ASTOR'S BEECHWOOD MANSION
Bellevue Ave., Newport, 401-846-3773
Actors give living history tours re-creating life in the Victorian era.

BELCOURT CASTLE
Bellevue Ave., Newport, 401-846-0669
Some 2,000 art treasures and antiques on display in a Louis XIII–style castle.

BLITHEWOLD MANSION AND GARDENS
Ferry Rd. (Rte. 114), Bristol, 401-253-2707
Acres of gardens include largest redwood tree east of the Rockies. The 45-room house has summer tours.

GILBERT STUART BIRTHPLACE
Gilbert Stuart Rd. (off Rte. 1A), North Kingstown, 401-294-3001
Birthplace of the American painter; tours of the house, a snuff mill, and a working waterfall (April–November).

GREEN ANIMALS
Cory's Ln., Portsmouth, 401-847-1000
Victorian-era topiary gardens overlooking Narragansett Bay.

JOHN BROWN HOUSE
Power St., Providence, 401-331-8575
Magnificent 18th-century mansion with fine examples of Rhode Island furniture, art, and silver.

NEWPORT MANSIONS
Preservation Society of Newport County, 401-847-1000
Ten properties, including the famous Vanderbilt "cottages," Marble House and the Breakers, plus several fine Colonial and Victorian mansions.

Other Resources

BLACKSTONE VALLEY TOURISM COUNCIL
401-724-2200

BLOCK ISLAND TOURISM COUNCIL
401-466-5200

NEWPORT COUNTY CONVENTION AND VISITORS BUREAU
401-849-8048

PROVIDENCE–WARWICK CONVENTION AND VISITORS BUREAU
Providence, 401-274-1636; Warwick, 401-738-2000, ext. 6402

RHODE ISLAND STATE COUNCIL ON THE ARTS
401-222-3880

SOUTH COUNTY TOURISM COUNCIL
401-789-4422

CREDITS

The authors have made every effort to reach copyright holders of text and owners of illustrations, and wish to thank those individuals and institutions that permitted the reprinting of text or the reproduction of works in their collections. Any omission is unintentional and appropriate credit will be given in future editions if such copyright holders contact the publisher. Credits not listed in the captions are provided below. References are to page numbers; the designations a, b, and c indicate position of illustrations on pages.

Text

"Rhode Island Is Famous for You," by Howard Dietz and Arthur Schwartz. Used by permission of Warner Brothers Publications

"Life Is Like a Musical Comedy," by George M. Cohan. Used by permission of George M. Cohan Music Publishing Company.

Illustrations

ADELSON GALLERIES, N.Y.: **22** *Old Homestead by the Sea.* Oil on canvas. 12⅝ x 22⅛"; AMERICAN HERITAGE: **26b**; ART RESOURCE, N.Y.: **8** *October Sundown, Newport, Rhode Island;* CHIHULY STUDIO: **84** Photo by Russell Johnson; CHRISTIE'S IMAGES: **5** Silk on silk needlework. 18 x 20½"; **9** Giltwood, eglomise, mirror. 38 x 22¼"; **60a; 61a;** CORBIS: **32a; 62b;** CULVER PICTURES: **88;** LEONARD HARRIS/STOCK BOSTON: **36b;** HASBRO, INC.: **86b;** HERRESHOFF MARINE MUSEUM: **17;** JOHNSON & WALES: **48b; 86a;** ALLISON LANGLEY/STOCK NEWPORT: **25;** LPW, INC.: **75a;** PENELOPE MANZELLA: **35** *Folding the Run.* Oil on linen. 46 x 40"; NATIONAL GEOGRAPHIC SOCIETY IMAGE COLLECTION: **12a** Rhode Island flag. Illustration by Marilyn Dye Smith; **12b** Violet and Rhode Island Red hen. Illustration by Robert Hynes; NEW ENGLAND PEST CONTROL: **87a;** NEWPORT ART MUSEUM: **2** *The Blue Porch.* Oil on canvas. 47½ x 35"; NEWPORT HISTORICAL SOCIETY: **16;** NEW YORK PUBLIC LIBRARY PICTURE COLLECTION: **29b; 47b;** OLD DARTMOUTH HISTORICAL SOCIETY, NEW BEDFORD WHALING MUSEUM, MA.: **40–41** Polychromed wood. 84" long; PHOTOFEST: **73;** REDWOOD LIBRARY AND ATHENAEUM, NEWPORT: **29a** *Mrs. Bannister and Her Son.* Oil on canvas. 36 x 30"; RHODE ISLAND HISTORICAL SOCIETY: **31** *Burning of the Gaspee.* Oil on canvas. 34½ x 54"; RHODE ISLAND SCHOOL OF DESIGN, MUSEUM OF ART: **27** Portrait of Ninigret II. Oil on canvas. 33½ x 30½". Gift of Mr. Robert Winthrop. Photo by Del Bogart; **37b** Silver with patinated, oxidized, and gilt decoration. 9½" high. The Gorham Collection. Gift of Textron, Inc. Photo by Cathy Carver; **43a** Painted pine; JIM SCHWABEL/NEW ENGLAND STOCK PHOTO: **89;** STOCK BOSTON: **59b** Photo by Susan Van Etten; ONNE VAN DER WAL/STOCK NEWPORT: **1; 21;** WADSWORTH ATHENEUM, HARTFORD: **23b** *The Old Fort, Conanicut Island.* Watercolor and gouache on paper. 24 x 38". Bequest of Ambrose Spencer